Food and Farming

Andrew Langley

Illustrated by M. Bergin, J. Field, J. James, B. Donohoe

Heinemann

HISTORY OF BRITAIN – FOOD AND FARMING
was produced for Heinemann Children's Reference
by Lionheart Books, London.

Editor: Lionel Bender
Designer: Ben White
Editorial Assistant: Madeleine Samuel
Picture Researcher: Jennie Karrach
Media Conversion and Typesetting: MW Graphics
Educational Consultant: Jane Shuter
Editorial Advisors: Andrew Farrow, Paul Shuter

Production Controller: David Lawrence

First published in Great Britain in 1997 by
Heinemann Educational Publishers, a division of Reed
Educational and Professional Publishing Limited,
Halley Court, Jordan Hill, Oxford OX2 8EJ.

MADRID ATHENS
FLORENCE PRAGUE WARSAW
PORTSMOUTH NH CHICAGO SAO PAULO MEXICO
SINGAPORE TOKYO MELBOURNE AUCKLAND
IBADAN GABORONE JOHANNESBURG KAMPALA NAIROBI

ISBN 0431 05723 0 Hb   ISBN 0431 05732 X Pb

British Library Cataloguing-in-Publication Data.
A catalogue record for this book is available
from the British Library.

Printed in Hong Kong by Wing King Tong Company Limited

Most of the artwork in this book has been published in other titles in the
History of Britain series.

Acknowledgements
Picture credits
Pages: 4: Michael Holford. 5: C. M. Dixon. 6: Lesley and Roy Adkins
Picture Library. 8-9: The Bridgeman Art Library/British Library, London
Add 42130 f.208. 9: Martyn F. Chillmaid. 10: The Bridgeman Art
Library/British Library, London. Add 42130 f.207. 11: Fotomas Index.
12: The Bridgeman Art Library/British Library, London. Add 18855
f.109. 13, 14: Fotomas Index. 15-16: © Crown Copyright, Historic Royal
Palaces. 16: Fotomas Index. 17: Michael Holford. 18: The National Trust
Photographic Library/Angelo Hornak. 19: Fotomas Index. 20-21: Fine Art
Photographic Library Ltd. 21: Mary Evans Picture Library/Illustrated
London News. 22: The National Trust Photographic Library/Will Curwen.
23: Mary Evans Picture Library/Illustrated London News. 24: Mary Evans
Picture Library. 25: Fine Art Photographic Library Ltd. 26: Hulton Deutsch
Collection Limited. 27: Robert Opie Collection. 28: Mary Evans Picture
Library. 28-29: Safeway Ltd plc.

Artwork credits
Main illustrators: Mark Bergin, John James, James Field.
Additional illustrations by Bill Donohoe.

Cover: Artwork by Mark Bergin, Bill Donohoe, John James and
Gerald Wood.

INTRODUCTION

There are three ways of getting enough to eat – hunting, growing or buying food. The first people to live in Britain were hunters. They gathered wild plants or killed game. Then came the first farmers, who grew their food. They planted crops and kept sheep and cattle. Later invaders introduced new and better ways of farming. Increasingly, people bought their food from others. In the 1600s, travellers to the New World of America brought back new kinds of food. But since Victorian times the population of Britain has been so big that farmers cannot grow enough to feed everyone. Today, Britain imports much of the food it needs.

CONTENTS

HUNTERS AND FARMERS

About 400,000 years ago, the first people came to Britain from Europe. They ate whatever food they could find. Some hunted deer and wild pigs. Some ate plant shoots and fruits. Others gathered shellfish from the seashore.

By about 6,000 BC, early Britons had made two great discoveries. One was that food tasted better when it was cooked over a fire. The second was a simple kind of farming. People began to clear patches in the woodland that covered much of Britain. They found that juicy young plants grew in these clearings. Deer and wild cattle came to feed there and were easier to catch.

The first proper farmers arrived in Britain in about 3,500 BC. They brought seeds for new plants, such as wheat and barley, which they sowed in clearings, and also sheep, pigs and goats.

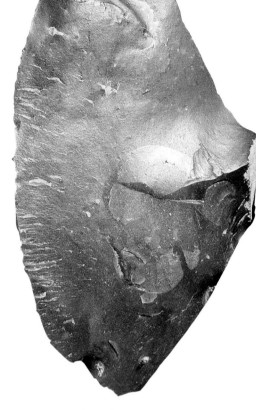

△ **A flintstone** used to scrape flesh from animals skins.

◁ **Hunters cut up a deer with knives made of flint**. They have killed their prey with spears or with arrows fired from bows. The arrows and spears have flint tips.

△ **Meat is cooked over a wood fire.** All the meat was eaten. The skin was used for clothing or shelters. The bones and horns were made into tools.

◁ **Early farmers** dig up ground for crops using wooden picks.

▷ **Wild pigs** and other animals were domesticated, or tamed, to keep on the farms.

Hunters had to wander in search of game, but farmers lived differently. They settled in one place and built houses. They cleared more land for crops, and put up fences to keep in their cattle. Men usually did the ploughing and looked after the animals. Women gathered wild food, such as nuts, and did the cooking. Everyone helped to harvest the crops.

◁ **A woman cooks** a stew of meat, water and herbs. The iron pot hangs over the fire from a hook. By the fire is a clay water pot.

◁ (Below) **A round hut on a farm** in about 500 BC. Farmers stored grain in pits nearby, to use in the winter.

▽ **The remains of a farm settlement** in Devon, from 650 BC.

VILLAS AND VINES

In AD 43 the Romans invaded Britain. They brought with them new farming tools and new kinds of food. During the next three centuries, the Romans built new towns and roads, too. And the invading army and the people in the new towns all had to be fed.

The Romans increased the area of farmland so that more crops could be grown. Even marshy areas were drained and ploughed up. Roman soldiers also raised their own farm animals at their forts, such as those along Hadrian's Wall.

▷ **Copies of Roman pottery tableware** and glassware, and various Roman foods.

▽ **A donkey turns a mill wheel** to crush wheat into flour.

△ **Fruit and vegetables** from local farms were sold in the towns. Shoppers could also buy fresh meat and bread. Some shops sold shellfish which were kept alive in tanks of water.

◁ **A Roman villa** was a farm, with a house and barns. Inside the villa walls were gardens with fruit trees and herbs. Outside were the fields for grain and vegetables.

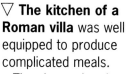

▽ **The kitchen of a Roman villa** was well equipped to produce complicated meals.
• The charcoal and wood fire is raised on a hearth of brick or stone.
• The cooking pot stands on a metal grid.
• Liquids, such as the popular garum (a fish sauce), are kept in jars.
• Vegetables and joints of meat are hung from hooks in the ceiling.
• Fresh water is carried in wooden buckets.

First course

Main course

Dessert

△ **A Roman three-course meal.**

◁ **At grand banquets,** guests ate lying on couches by the table. They used knives and spoons, or picked with their fingers. The meal might start with peacock eggs, stuffed olives and oysters. The main course might be boar's head, roast chicken and lobster. For dessert, there might be fruit, cakes and stuffed dates.

How do we know what people ate in Roman Britain? We can look at what they left behind. The bones of cattle, sheep and pigs have been found near army forts, showing that soldiers ate a lot of meat. They also loved shellfish. A pile of a million oyster shells was discovered at Silchester in Hampshire.

Wealthy Romans kept many unusual animals for food. Peacocks and pheasants, brought from Italy, were bred in pens. Dormice were put in special pots and fattened up with acorns and nuts. Snails were kept on tiny islands in ponds, so that they could not escape.

The Romans introduced many new kinds of vegetables and fruits to Britain. Among them were cabbages, onions, lettuce and turnips. The first orchards of apple and pear trees were planted by the Romans. But the invaders' favourite fruit was grapes. Grape pips have been found at many Roman sites, and there are several remains of vineyards in southern England. Most grapes were used to make wine, though huge loads of wine, in barrels or clay jars, were also carried by ship from France and Spain.

Hard Work on the Farm

After the Romans left, Britain was split up among invaders from Ireland and Northern Europe. In England, Saxon kings shared out the best farmland among their most powerful warriors, or thanes, who in turn rented their land to peasant farmers, or churls.

Most churls rented a 'hide' of land – an area big enough to grow food for one family. Three or four of these family farms were grouped together. Some churls settled on farmland seized from the Britons. Others had to clear wood-land and plough up new land for crops.

▷ **A Saxon monastery** of about AD 700. The monks had their own farm. There are fruit and vegetables in the gardens at the front. Cattle are kept in the sheds, and chickens in coops.

◁ **Saxon farmers** had to work hard all year round to grow enough food. Their main crops were wheat, oats and barley. They also grew peas, beans and lentils. In some years, the crops might fail because of drought. Cattle and sheep might die because of disease. Viking raiders might steal the food stores. Starvation was a constant threat.

◁ **A woman cooking in Jorvik** (York) in 870.

▷ **Viking settlers** often lived near the shore. They caught fish and preserved it by salting it or drying it in the open (far right).

Pigs, which then were thinner than modern breeds, were useful animals for Saxon farmers. They could live on rough land. The pigs were allowed to wander in the woods, where they ate nuts and roots. Goats were also happy there, eating leaves and brambles. But cattle and sheep needed young grass to eat. The farmers kept them on pasture land, which had been cleared of trees. Farmers had little winter food for cattle, so many of them were killed in the autumn.

Saxon farmers also used animals to help them. Oxen were yoked together in teams to pull the wheeled ploughs over the fields. Horses pulled the carts full of hay and other crops. Dogs guarded the sheep from wolves at night. Shepherds tied their dogs by ropes to their belts. If a dog saw a wolf, it would jerk at the rope and wake the shepherd.

▽ **A replica of foods in a Viking kitchen.** There are seabird eggs, dried meats and fish, bread and milk.

▽ **A 14th century illustration** showing a lord dining with his family at a long wooden table. A servant brings in dishes of food. On the table are bowls, plates, knives, spoons, bread and eggs. Forks were not yet used for eating.

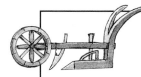

COMBATTING STARVATION

In medieval times, nine out of ten British people worked on the land. They had to. People were only able to grow the food they needed, and rarely had any to spare that they could sell or barter for other goods.

Most people were peasants, who lived in villages. All land in a village belonged to the lord of the manor. The peasants were bound to work for him, tilling his fields and harvesting his crops. In return, the lord gave them land for their own food.

▷ **Every village or manor** in Norman times had to grow all the food it needed. Only salt (used for preserving meat in winter) was bought from outside.

▷ **Stewing meat over a fire and chopping vegetables** – part of a medieval book illustration.

▽ **Domesday Book,** begun in 1086, was a survey of England. The king's officers visited villages, finding out who held each area of land and how it was used. Domesday Book showed that about two-thirds of the country was used for raising crops and animals.

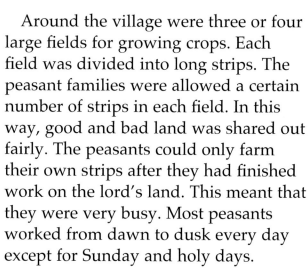

Around the village were three or four large fields for growing crops. Each field was divided into long strips. The peasant families were allowed a certain number of strips in each field. In this way, good and bad land was shared out fairly. The peasants could only farm their own strips after they had finished work on the lord's land. This meant that they were very busy. Most peasants worked from dawn to dusk every day except for Sunday and holy days.

▷ **Peasants kept their animals fenced-off** in their houses. They stored hay and straw to feed the animals in winter. In summer, farm animals grazed on common land.

▽ **A boy scares birds** to stop them eating the seed in the newly-sown fields.

▷ **Wool became a valuable product** in medieval times. The fleeces were cut from sheep in early summer.

▽ **A woman spins thread** from wool while her husband breaks up the soil for sowing seeds.

△ **People ate food from wooden bowls** or sometimes from just thick pieces of bread, and drank ale or cider from leather mugs. They used knives to cut up bread and meat, and spoons made from cow's horns for pottage.

△ **Peasant food was simple.** Pottage, a thick broth with vegetables or meat, was served at most meals. So was bread, made from dark, coarse flour. The Church ordered that no-one should eat meat on three days each week.

Most cottages had only one room, and all cooking was done over a fire on a flat stone in the centre. Peasants baked their bread on small stones in the fire. Meat was usually boiled in an iron pot, but small animals, such as pigeons or even squirrels, were covered with clay and cooked in the hot ashes.

THE GARDEN GROWS

The most important animal in Tudor Britain was the sheep. By 1500, there were over 8 million sheep on the land – far more than people! Sheep were not kept for their meat, but for their wool, which was valuable.

△ **Wine in barrels.**

Rich farmers wanted more land for their sheep flocks. So they began to enclose the old open fields with hedges or fences. This meant that the villagers often had less land to grow crops or feed their animals. But in many areas farming life had hardly changed. Some farmers still dragged thorn bushes across ploughed fields to break up the soil. When its crop had been grown, a field was left fallow, or wild, for a whole year.

▽ **A village in late-Tudor times** (compare it with the picture on page 10). Can you see
• the windmill, where the wheat and barley were ground into flour;
• the fences round the enclosed fields in the distance;
• the shepherd tending his flock of sheep;
• the vegetable garden behind the church;
• the tithe barn below the church? (All villagers had to give a tithe, or tenth, of their produce to the Church. It was stored in the big tithe barn.)

▽ **Many different animals were killed for meat**, such as deer, rabbits and pigeons.

▽ **In winter,** many animals were killed and preserved in salt in wooden barrels.

▽ **Herbs and spices** were used in cooking to cover the rotten taste of old meat.

▷ **Sheep shearing on a Tudor farm** – from an illustrated manuscript of about 1540. Sheep were kept for meat as well as wool. As there were no freezers, food had to be preserved so that it would last a long time. Most meats were salted or 'smoked' by hanging them in a chimney. Eggs were covered with wax and buried in sawdust. Milk was made into cheese.

△ **Poor people** ate coarse bread (often made from acorns), with butter, eggs and bacon, and drank ale or cider.

△ **Rich people** ate bread made with white flour, and sweetened their food with sugar. They drank wine.

△ **Town-workers** mostly lived, slept, cooked and ate in the same room. Soup and meat was cooked over an open fire. Breakfast, of bread and soup or meat, was eaten early. Lunch was often bought in a tavern or from a nearby 'cookshop'. Supper, in the early evening, was usually bread and cheese with ale.

△ **A rich family eats together.** In poor families, the husband would eat only when the day's work was done.

By the end of the sixteenth century, there were many more vegetable and fruit gardens. Every country house had garden beds for beetroot, parsnips and onions. New fruits from Europe and Asia, such as quinces and apricots, were trained against walls.

Herbs were important to give flavour to dishes and as medicines. Gardeners laid out herb beds in knot patterns, decorated with flowers. Only the wealthy could afford spices, such as cloves, which came from the Far East.

13

ROYAL FEASTS

Tudor kings and queens ate splendid food – and spent thousands of pounds on it. When Henry VIII was with his court at Nonsuch Palace, there were 1,500 followers and servants to feed each day. Nobles also had to provide food for their large households.

All this cooking needed many people (Elizabeth I's kitchens had a staff of over 160). And it took up a lot of space. Each great Tudor house had its own kitchens (for cooking and preparing food), larders (for storing food), cellars (for keeping wine), dairy and bakehouse. At feasts, most of the diners sat in the great hall, the largest room in the house. But the lord, his family and important friends ate together in a private room.

◁ **Monasteries** had been centres of farming as well as religion for nearly 1,000 years. But in 1536, Henry VIII began to dissolve, or close down, the monasteries. He made a fortune selling church land and used much of it to pay for his grand houses and big feasts.

◁ (Inset) **Monks** eat a simple meal together in the monastery refectory.

△ **Henry VIII hunting with his hawk.** The hawk was released to catch rabbits and partridges. Hunting was a popular sport for noblemen (and women – Elizabeth I often rode after deer). The game, including herons, hares and even swans, was often served at feasts.

◁ **'The House of Rest'.** This Tudor illustration shows a merchant sitting down to a meal at an inn. The inn-keeper's wife cooks meat over the fire. Inns provided the monarch's followers with places to eat, drink and sleep along the way when they moved from one palace to another.

△ **Stuffed peacock,** one of the grand dishes enjoyed by Tudor monarchs.

▷ **Henry VIII dines in his chamber.** Servants bring in food and musicians play.

At a royal feast, guardsmen might carry in as many as twenty dishes for every course. Each guard was given a mouthful to eat, to make sure that none of the food was poisoned. After the main meal came the 'banquet' – a colourful course of sweets, such as animals made of sugar and marzipan. Special banqueting houses were built on roofs or in gardens.

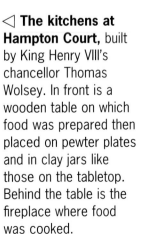

◁ **The kitchens at Hampton Court,** built by King Henry VIII's chancellor Thomas Wolsey. In front is a wooden table on which food was prepared then placed on pewter plates and in clay jars like those on the tabletop. Behind the table is the fireplace where food was cooked.

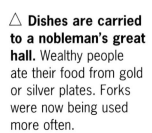

△ **Dishes are carried to a nobleman's great hall.** Wealthy people ate their food from gold or silver plates. Forks were now being used more often.

NEW WORLD, NEW FOOD

During Tudor and Stuart times, European explorers found new sea routes to America and the Far East. They brought back many kinds of food. From America came sweetcorn, pumpkins, potatoes and chocolate. From the Far East came tea and spices.

At first, British settlers in North America found farming hard, and many of them starved. They had to learn how to catch game and grow crops like the Indians.

▷ **An early British colony in North America.** Like the first settlers in Britain, these pioneers had to clear fields to sow crops.

▷ **A ship carrying settlers to America.**

▷ (Centre) **Turkeys and corn** were two New World foods which were brought to Europe.

▷ (Far right) **Tobacco from America** made smoking fashionable.

▽ **In the early 17th century,** King James I wrote a pamphlet against the practice of smoking tobacco.

▷ **Unloading food at a new settlement** in America. Until settlers could grow enough crops and tame animals, they had to bring food from Britain.

The seas around the east coast of North America contained huge numbers of fish, especially cod. Fishermen from Britain and other European countries crossed the Atlantic to catch them. The fish was salted and packed in barrels during the voyage home. Cod became a more important food in Britain – and still is today.

◁ **Sailors from Bristol** fishing with nets for the cod which swarmed in the shallow seas off the coast of Newfoundland (Canada).

▽ **Many new crops** were brought from South America, including coffee and potatoes. Potatoes, probably brought by Francis Drake, were soon grown in Scotland and Ireland, becoming the main food crop there. Tomatoes did not become popular until much later.

▷ **African slaves** were brought to the West Indies to work on sugar plantations.

▽ **Sugar cane from the West Indies** was shipped to Britain, where it was refined. The sugar was sold in big pieces. It was used in fruit dishes.

During the seventeenth century, British explorers and merchants began making longer voyages in search of new lands and trade. They needed to take a large supply of food which would last many weeks without spoiling. The most usual rations were salted beef, dried peas and bread. Some took smoked hams covered in honey or pine tar to keep out air and flies (and pork fat was used as a kind of sun cream!). Live hens provided eggs, and goats gave fresh milk.

A FARMING REVOLUTION

Between 1700 and 1850, the population of Britain soared from 9 million to 28 million. The reason for this was more food. Improved methods of farming allowed greater quantities and quality of food to be produced. As a result, food was cheaper to buy.

Farmers found new ways of making their land more fertile. They put marl (a kind of clay) on light soil to make it hold greater amounts of water. They grew clover and special grasses, which added goodness to the soil. And they hoed between the rows of crops to keep down weeds.

An important new crop was turnips. In winter, cattle and sheep were put on to turnip fields to feed. This, with better hay and grain, solved the problem of keeping animals through the winter. Now, far fewer had to be killed. Also, by careful breeding, farmers could rear better cattle, sheep and pigs.

△ **Jethro Tull built the first seed** drill in about 1701. This sowed seeds directly into the soil in rows. Before this, the seed had been scattered by hand, and a lot of it had been wasted.

▽ **A Hereford bull** – an improved breed of cattle. Fatter and healthier cattle like this were bred by pioneer farmers, such as Robert Bakewell of Leicestershire. He chose only the best animals in his herd to breed together. Sheep and pig breeds were also improved in this way to provide more meat.

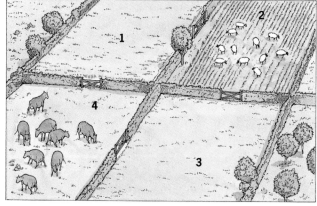

△ **The 'four-course' system of rotating crops.** For centuries, farmers had used only three courses. They had grown wheat one year, barley the next, and then left the field fallow, or empty, for a year to regain its fertility. The new system avoided this waste and used land all the time.

Year 1: Wheat, sowed in the autumn. **Year 2:** Turnips, used to feed cattle and sheep in winter. **Year 3:** Barley, sowed in the spring. **Year 4:** Grass and clover for cattle and sheep to graze on. The dung from the animals made the soil more fertile.

▽ **Farm workers plant a hedge** and enclose a field. People who lived on common land were forced to move out.

◁ **The Fens** (marshes) in Lincolnshire were drained, using windmills to pump away the water. The soil here was rich and ideal for growing grain and vegetables.

◁ **Turnips** were not the only winter feed. By 1800, many farmers were also giving cattle 'cake' made from crushed oil seeds.

The new farming changed the countryside, especially in England. Landowners had started to enclose, or fence off, the old open fields in Tudor times. Now enclosure speeded up. Between 1760 and 1815, over one million hectares of land were fenced with walls or hedges.

Villagers and small farmers had always used the common land for grazing their pigs, sheep and geese. Enclosure ruined their way of life and forced many to move to towns to find work. But it also made farming more efficient. Fences stopped animals from trampling on crops and spreading pests and diseases.

△ **Shepherds** use poles to push a flock of sheep into a stream in early summer. The men in the water are washing the fleeces of the sheep to clean them before they are shorn.

▷ **Laws allowing the enclosing of land,** and other new farming methods, threatened many people with losing their jobs. During the 1830s, protesters burned hayricks and smashed farm machines.

MACHINES ON THE FARM

"A curious, shapeless thing, with a man riding upon it, comes jerking forward, tearing its iron teeth deep through the earth." This was how Richard Jefferies described the sight of a steam plough in the 1870s. New machines like this revolutionized farming.

△ **Hand-power – a harvester** cuts down wheat with a sickle, which he keeps very sharp.

▽ (Bottom) **Wheat** is fed into the top of a steam powered thresher.

▽ **Machine-power – a steam plough** is pulled across the field by chains driven by a stationary steam engine.

The first all-steel plough had been built in 1837. It was still pulled by horses but was stronger than the old wooden plough. Its blade stayed sharp and did not get clogged with mud. Then iron rollers were introduced, to crush the lumps of soil, and chain harrows broke them up into smaller pieces.

During the 1850s, farmers began using horse-drawn reapers to cut down corn. Steam-powered threshers separated the grain from the straw. By the 1870s, the first steam tractors were at work.

△ **Horse-drawn carts** were still vital for moving all kinds of loads on the farm, such as cow and pig manure for the fields.

◁ **A horse pulling a cart** piled high with wheat from a harvest field. Children still worked as farm-hands.

Other inventions improved farmland, making it grow better crops. The 'mole plough' was dragged under the earth to make drainage channels in wet ground. Clay pipes made draining even simpler.

Scientists studied the way plants grew, and found that some chemicals present in animal bones and manure enriched the soil. Soon many farmers were using new fertilizers. Among these was seabird dung, called guano, which was imported from South America.

△ **A bustling market** in Lambeth, London, in 1872. The populations of towns were growing fast, and needed a huge amount of food.

◁ **Steam ploughs** only worked well on big, flat fields. On smaller farms, horses were used to pull ploughs until well into the twentieth century.

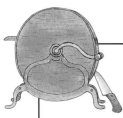

FRESH AND PRESERVED FOOD

By the 1850s, most British people could eat a bigger variety of food than ever before. Farms and gardens were growing more. Railways carried fresh food swiftly from the countryside to the towns. And new ways of milling and baking had made bread cheaper.

The revolution in farming soon spread into the gardens of homes. There, people could use fertilizers, lawn-mowers and hoses. Many new houses were built with space for a vegetable plot. But the most magnificent gardens of all served the big country houses. Sheltered by high walls, these gardens produced vegetables, fruit and flowers all the year round.

▽ **Goods are being loaded on to a train.** Railways could carry fresh milk and other farm produce to the towns every day.

△ **The high walls** round the huge kitchen garden at Wallington in Northumberland kept warmth in and winds out, helping plants grow more quickly. The glasshouses were heated in winter with hot water flowing through pipes.

▷ **A gardener** delivers a basket of fresh vegetables to a kitchen maid to prepare. All the house's fruit and vegetables were grown in the walled garden. In winter, apples, pears and other fruit were stored in a special shed. A garden like this needed a staff of 20 or more men and boys to keep it running. They grew an amazing variety of crops. Catalogues from the 1880s list 60 different kinds of peas, and over 500 different kinds of apple trees!

▷ **Food was usually cheaper to buy** in the towns than in country villages. City market stalls and shops competed with each other to gain customers, and kept their prices low.

▷ **Experiments with tinned food** were made in about 1817. Food was sealed in cans then heated to kill germs. In 1856, the Royal Navy set up its own canning factory to supply meat and vegetables for sailors.

◁ **Some cows were kept in the cities** and their milk was sold fresh each day.

△ **A shopkeeper** with a tin of biscuits. Many processed foods had colourful packages.

Meanwhile, people found new ways to preserve foods. The earliest freezers were 'ice houses', where food was packed in ice hacked from frozen ponds in winter. By 1880, meat was being sent to Britain from America in chilled containers. Mutton (sheep meat) sealed in cans came from Australia. Shoppers could also buy food that had not been grown on farms but made in factories. Custard powder, self-raising flour, margarine, dried soup and bottles of sauce were among the first of these 'processed' foods.

RICH, POOR OR MIDDLE-CLASS?

In 1864, a doctor wrote: "In very poor families, the children are fed at breakfast and supper chiefly with bread. At dinner they have the same food or boiled potato or cabbage." These people had no stove or running water for preparing and cooking food.

▽ **A menu** showing what people might have eaten at a grand formal dinner, such as the one drawn by Richard Doyle in 1864 (bottom). This picture, called *A State Party*, shows Queen Victoria (seen from behind), government ministers, rich guests, waiters and poor onlookers.

At the same time, richer people could afford much better food. At dinner parties, they showed off their wealth by serving expensive and complicated dishes. By the 1880s, this meal might consist of twelve courses, including soup, fish, meat and three different desserts.

In between the rich and poor were the middle classes. They were better off than ever before, and wanted to copy the eating habits of the wealthy. The middle classes did not grow their own food but bought it from shops or from the traders who sold vegetables and fish at the door.

△ **Afternoon tea** was a new kind of meal for wealthy or middle-class families. They drank tea and ate thin sandwiches, cakes and biscuits.

MENU
Potage à la Reine.
Saumon.
Côtelette de Veau.
Pommes de terre.
Petits Pois.
Charlotte Russe.

△ **Mealtimes** for middle-class Victorians were formal – and filling!
• Breakfasts might include pies, meat, eggs and muffins

• Lunch was lighter, with cold meats and salads
• Dinner started at 8 pm. Meat was put on a dish in the kitchen then brought to the table to be carved.

▷ **Working-class** Victorians had simple meals. Dinner might be cold meat slices, bread and butter, and tea.

▽ **Most Victorians were religious** and usually said 'Grace' before meals, as this painting shows.

At the beginning of the Victorian Age, many kitchens had a cast-iron 'range' for cooking. This had an open coal fire with an oven next to it. By the 1850s, many people were using the new closed range, which had a hot-plate over the fire. Gas began to replace coal for heating.

Gadgets made the cook's life much easier. Food could be kept fresh in early refrigerators, which were special large cupboards packed with ice. Other useful Victorian inventions were mincers, coffee grinders, knife sharpeners, food mixers and bread slicers. The very first tea-making machine, attached to an alarm clock, was built in 1891.

WAR AND RATIONING

By 1914, the population of the British Isles had risen to over 43 million. Farmers could not grow enough to feed this many people, so a lot of food had to be bought from abroad by ship. For example, three-quarters of the wheat for bread was imported.

△ **Ration books** were issued to everyone at the start of the Second World War. The coupons inside were cut out when an item was purchased.

▽ **Plenty of fresh food** is being grown in this 1940s suburban garden. There are chickens, as well as vegetables, herbs and fruit trees.

During the First World War (1914 – 1918), the German Navy attacked and sank many ships carrying food to Britain. Several kinds of food began to run short. By 1917, there was only enough food to last the country for three weeks. The government limited the amount of meat, flour and other foods that people could buy. This was called rationing.

When the Second World War broke out in 1939, rationing began right away. Among the first foods to be rationed were butter, meat and fresh eggs.

▽ **Growing vegetables** on an allotment set up in 1942 on the site of a house destroyed by a German bomb. Crops were grown on every available piece of land.

26

▽ **An adult's weekly ration of food** (below right) included 4 ounces (112 grams) of butter, 14 old pence-worth (about £2 today) of meat, and 12 ounces (336 grams) of sugar.

▽ **Queuing to buy food.** The government urged people to buy preserved food, such as dried eggs.

△ **From 1942, many soldiers from the USA** arrived in Britain to help fight the war. They had stores of many things that were rationed. This soldier has brought an English family presents of chocolate and sugar.

During 1942, the Germans sank 8 million tonnes of shipping. Food was again running dangerously short. Besides rationing, the British government encouraged people to 'Dig For Victory'. Extra land, including parks and playing fields, was ploughed up to grow crops. People grew vegetables instead of flowers in their gardens.

▷ **Hundreds of city shops were damaged** or destroyed by German bombs during raids known as the Blitz. But people were determined to keep going. Shop-keepers patched up broken windows and walls and put up signs saying 'Business as Usual'.

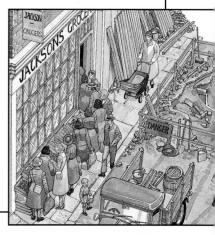

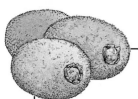

FACTORY FARMS, FAST FOOD

The Second World War was good for British farmers. People saw how important it was to grow as much food as possible at home. Since the war, farmers have been helped by government money to become more efficient, with new machines, methods and chemicals.

Today, everything is done on a big scale. Huge tractors haul wide ploughs and cultivators. Tonnes of fertilizer (made in factories) are spread over the land. Drills sow twelve or more lines of seeds at the same time. Chemical sprays kill off the weeds.

Vast combine harvesters are used to cut down the crop, separate the grains and throw out the straw at the back. To make room for such monster machines, hedges and walls have been ripped out.

▽ **This chemical sprayer** stretches for 6 metres on each side of the tractor. Grain from these vast fields is stored in the tall silo in the background.

△ **An advertisement for an electric refrigerator,** from 1951. At this time, only a few Britons could afford a 'fridge'. Today, most homes have one. Modern homes have other kitchen gadgets, too. Freezers, microwave ovens, toasters, electric kettles and food mixers have all helped to make cooking easier, quicker and cleaner than ever before.

▷ **Cans of food on a factory line.** Factories like this can process huge amounts of food without stopping. The food is cleaned, prepared and partly cooked. Then it is put into the cans, sealed and heated to a high temperature to complete the cooking and destroy germs.

In spite of this farming revolution, a lot
of Britain's food comes from overseas.
There are many ways of preserving meat,
fish, vegetables and fruit so that they can
be sent cheaply over long distances
without 'going off', or rotting, on the
way. Frozen, canned or dried food will
last for many months. Most preserved
food contains extra chemicals that
prevent harmful germs from developing.
Some people think that these chemicals
are themselves a danger to health.

Much fresh food also comes from
abroad. Aircraft carry vegetables and
fruit in chilled compartments across the
world in a few hours. This kind of food
goes rotten very quickly, so some of it is
treated with special light to stop decay.
In spite of this costly treatment, imported
food can be cheaper than home-grown
produce. In 1997, strawberries from
California cost less than English ones!

△ **Most eggs in Britain**
are laid by hens kept in
cages with wire floors
and no natural light.
Their eggs roll on to a
conveyor belt that takes
them away to be packed.
Other farm animals, such
as pigs, sometimes
spend their whole lives in
heated concrete sheds.

△ **Many people
believe that this
'factory farming'** is
cruel and that the drugs
given to some farm
animals to 'fatten them
up' harm those people
who eat their meat. For
safety, some farmers
now allow hens to roam
'free range' over a field.

△ **The most popular
'meal'** in Britain is 'fast
food' – such as the
American beef burger.
Burgers from shops are
quick to buy and easy
to eat. Along with chips
and sugary drinks, this
kind of food is fattening
and may encourage
heart disease.

PLACES TO VISIT

Here are some sites relating to food and farming in Britain. Your local Tourist Office will be able to tell you about other places in your area.

Acton Scott Historic Working Farm, Shropshire. Shows the way people farmed in Victorian times.
Baxters of Speyside, Grampian. Find out how soup and haggis are made on a guided tour of a food factory.
Butser Farm, Hampshire. A reconstructed Iron Age farm.
Chedworth Villa, Gloucestershire. Remains of a Roman villa showing the kitchen area.
Chesters Fort, Hexham. A well-preserved Roman cavalry fort with eating and kitchen area.
Erddig, Clwyd. Eighteenth-century house with perfectly preserved kitchens.
Felin Crewi Watermill, Powys. A working water-powered flour mill.
Haddon Hall, Derbyshire. Includes a grand medieval banqueting hall.
Hampton Court Palace, Surrey. Has magnificent Tudor kitchens.
Jorvik Viking Centre, York. Excavated city shows how the Vikings cooked and ate, among many other things.
Longleat House, Wiltshire. Contains a perfect Victorian kitchen.

Museum of London, London. Many exhibits show Londoners' eating habits through history.
North of England Open Air Museum, Tyne and Wear. A recreated town from around 1913.
Skara Brae, Orkney. Stone Age village which shows how people lived and ate.
Ulster History Park, Co. Tyrone. Reconstructions of Ulster life from 8000 BC.
West Stow, Suffolk. Reconstruction of an Anglo-Saxon village.

FURTHER READING

Here are some books that will tell you more about the history of food and farming in Britain. You will find these, and others, in your local or school library.

The British Kitchen by Doreen Yarwood, Batsford, 1981.
The Field Guide: A Farmland Companion by John Woodward and Peter Luff, Blandford, 1983.
Food in England by Dorothy Hartley, Macdonald, first published in 1954.
A Taste of History: 10,000 Years of Food in Britain by Peter Brears and others, English Heritage/British Museum, 1993.

GLOSSARY

bakehouse A room or building where bread is baked in ovens.

banquet Usually a grand meal, with lots of food.

barley A grain crop used for food and for making beer and whisky.

Britons People who were living in Britain before the Roman and Saxon invasions.

class The group in society that a person belongs to. In the past, these were (in order from the highest, or richest): nobles, gentry, craftsmen, yeomen, peasants, the poor. Today, the order is: upper class, middle class and lower, or working, class.

colony Land in one country that is ruled by another country.

common land Land which is not owned by anyone, and which can be used by everyone.

cookshop A shop where cooked food can be bought.

cultivator A farming tool used instead of a plough, which breaks up the soil without turning it.

dairy The place on a farm where milk is stored. Here the cream is taken off the milk and made into cheese.

dessert The last course in a lunch or dinner, usually a sweet.

enclosure The fencing in of open common land with hedges and walls.

famine A disastrous shortage of food.

fertilizer A substance put on the soil which gives plants the right foods and chemicals to help them grow.

fleece The wool of a sheep.

flint A hard mineral that can be split to make a sharp edge.

game Wild animals hunted for food or sport.

glasshouse A building covered with glass for growing plants in; it lets in light but keeps the plants warm.

import To bring in goods, such as food, from another country.

lord A noble or king, a person who was owed loyalty by his followers.

merchant A person who makes their living by buying and selling things, either in their own country or abroad.

monarch The ruler of a country – the king or queen.

monastery A place where monks live together after taking religious vows.

peasant A farmer or labourer who works on the land.

plantation A large farm growing one crop, such as sugarcane or bananas.

range A cooking stove with surfaces and ovens on which you can cook several things at once.

rationing The sharing out of goods, especially food, which are in short supply so that everyone gets an equal share.

sickle A tool with a short, curved blade using for cutting grain or tall grass.

slave A person held captive and forced to work for no pay.

taxes Money collected by a lord or the government from the people, to pay for new roads, buildings or to equip an army.

tilling Preparing the soil for growing crops.

villa A large country house with a farm.

vineyard A field where grapevines are grown.

wheat A grain used for making bread, cakes and pasta.

working class People who were seen as poor and unimportant in Victorian times. These people had to work for others to earn a living – they were employees. Miners, shopworkers, servants, factory workers were working class.

INDEX